The Power of P-M-S:
Praise-Meditation-Study

By
Alicia Middleton

P.O. BOX 177
Tobyhanna, PA 18466
(973) 348-5067

Copyright © 2016 Alicia LaRaine Middleton
Shar Shey Publishing Company LLC
ISBN: 13: 978-0997266856
ISBN: 10: 0997266856
Book Cover Designed by: Dynastys CoverMe
Edited and Interior by: Latarsha Banks

All rights reserved. No part of this book may be reproduced or transmitted in any form or by any means, electronic or mechanical, including photocopying, recording, or by any information storage and retrieval system, without permission in writing from the copyright owner. This book was printed in the United States of America.

I DEDICATE THIS: TO MY LORD & SAVIOR
My husband, Rev. PK Middleton – my children Ahrayalab
Simon and Alema Isabelle
My parents: The late Deacon Oscar Simon Jenkins, Jr
Deaconess Evelyn Isabelle Jenkins
My sister Aunita Wilson
Nephews: Earle Jerreau, Marlon, Isaiah
AND TO ALL WHO HAVE SHARED IN THIS JOURNEY

ABOUT MY TESTIMONIES

Each testimony I have depicts how I applied the Power of P-M-S (Praise-Meditation-Study) throughout my life as a daughter, sister, aunt, niece, cousin, friend, secretary, teacher, mother, wife, minister, Co-Pastor and Doctorate of Education candidate. The above picture reminds me of the daily struggles I've experienced throughout my life and having the ability to smile as I overcame them all. The picture was taken in 2010 when I could not stand...let alone walk. I had to wear this back brace daily to prevent any sudden movements that would inflict excruciating pain. Today, I am on a journey to obtain the highest form of education to man and continue onto higher heights with God.

As a result, I have been compelled and counseled to share MY JOURNEY OF DELIVERANCE THROUGH DYSFUNCTION ON THE PATH TO MY DESTINATION.

The Power of P-M-S (Praise-Meditation-Study) will share my most personal, intimate P-M-S moments of my life from childhood to now and how I applied the word of God to deliver and mold me into the woman I am today!

Please be advised that these devotionals are personal and intimate moments I've experienced (past and present). For the sake of confidentiality, I will not share names, and if you may know the names of those I speak of, I ask that you do the same.

Alicia Middleton

WEEK 1

~ (John 16:33) ~
I have said these things to you, that in me you may have peace. In the world, you will have tribulation. But take heart; I have overcome the world.

When I lost my first baby, I immediately fell into a deep depression asking God, "Why did He forsake me". I wanted answers from Him. One day I was on 42nd Street, I observed a group of people discussing biblical scriptures informing who I was in Christ. Were these the answers I was looking for? For an entire year, I attended their bible study groups and worshiped with them on Sabbath. It was during this time that I began studying with the High Priest. He was going through a difficult time in his life. He informed me that his first child was taken from him by the mother and his current fiancée left him and moved to Canada. We began comforting one another through scriptures and I can honestly say that during this time, I began to hear God talking to me. However, as time passed I began to become confused with many of the scriptures he was sharing

The Power of P-M-S: Praise-Meditation-Study

with me and began feeling that many of the scriptures were being misconstrued as a benefit to himself.

As our relationship progressed, we were considering marriage, and it was during this time that he informed me that his fiancée returned and was pregnant. My spirit was perplexed because I discovered that I was pregnant as well. He began to slowly drift away from our relationship, using scriptures of biblical men having more than one wife as justification for his actions. Due to the fact that I was coming out of my depression, I did not want to anger God by questioning these scriptures and continued with our relationship. However, things were not getting any better between us. Therefore, I finally got the courage to leave but soon discovered I was pregnant again with my second child. As a result, I fought to continue this relationship for a couple of years but decided to leave for good. He reciprocated by calling me the devil and abandoned his two children. Once again, I was left alone and depression began to creep back in.

Alicia Middleton

This experience has taught me that in the world you will meet many tribulations, but in God, you will overcome! Just put your trust in Him and study His word and He will give you the answers you need!

WEEK 1 – POWER OF P-M-S STUDY

I AM AN OVERCOMER!

PRAISE: Thank you Lord, for in You I have found my peace!

MEDITATION: Teach me to learn that the world's ways are not your ways!

STUDY: *~John 16:33~I have said these things to you, that in me you may have peace. In the world you will have tribulation. But take heart; I have overcome the world.*

STEPS

How can you overcome the world with God's peace?
Do not let depression overcome you and become your downfall.
Let God envelope your heart with His peace and it will sustain you.

The Power of P-M-S: Praise-Meditation-Study

Alicia Middleton

WEEK 2

~ *(John 12:24)* ~
*Most assuredly, I say to you, unless a grain of wheat falls
into the ground and dies,
it remains alone; but if it dies, it produces much grain.*

Don't be dismayed by what you think may have ended or died. Your destination, your dream is taking root unseen. KEEP THE FAITH, STAY STRONG & BELIEVE THAT YOUR SETBACK IS A SET-UP FOR A GRAND COME-BACK!

In 2009, my career in education appeared to have died. After working for over twenty-four years with an impeccable record, I was being challenged by a new incoming principal and was forced to transfer from East Harlem to a school in the Bronx. After working for a little over a year, I began having pains in my back. I could not sit nor walk for any length of time. As the pain became increasingly worse, I knew it was time for me to see a doctor.

The Power of P-M-S: Praise-Meditation-Study

I was diagnosed with early onset osteoporosis and degenerative back disease. As a result, I had to go on an intermittent family medical leave for extensive rehab, three times a week. The symptoms were not getting better, and my principal began putting letters in my file for attendance. Although I was eligible for this leave, I was referred to our Medical Bureau for an exam to determine if I was fit to continue working. With an impeccable record, I could not understand why this was happening to me at such an early age. The results of the exam concluded that I was not fit to continue working, which forced me to retire because I was physically unable to work. Despite these results, mentally and spiritually I knew it was not over.

WEEK 2 – POWER OF P-M-S STUDY

What in your life appears dead?

PRAISE: My setback was a set up to position me for an *AWEmazing* comeback...

Alicia Middleton

MEDITATION: What is appearing to be your disability? Begin focusing on the promises of God. More than likely the promises do not align with what appears disabling. It is time to meditate, pray and bring it to God. Ask him to guide you into revealing **HIS** plan in bringing to life what you think has died.

STUDY: ~ (John 12:24) ~ Most assuredly, I say to you unless a grain of wheat falls into the ground and dies, it remains alone; but if it dies, it produces much grain.

STEPS

Write a synopsis of your story and list some steps you will take to overcome!

_____

_____

_____

_____

_____

_____

The Power of P-M-S: Praise-Meditation-Study

WEEK 3

~Psalms 46:10 ~
Be still, and know that I am God; I will be exalted among the nations,
I will be exalted in the earth!

What does it mean to be still? As for me, it definitely did not mean being complacent or motionless. Many times, I thought I was to do absolutely nothing. I would just sleep my day away. In doing so, my physical being began to get depressed. God sent a fire deep within my spirit that could not be contained. There was an anxiety within me that medication could not cure. It was impossible to remain still. I had to move, to take action. Let this be a reminder that being still does not mean being immobile. Being still simply means, allowing God to direct your movement for without HIM nothing is possible. Often times, we want to take the credit ourselves and move on our own accord.

Being still simply means allowing God control of your movements. Being still also means going into your worship closet. Taking time to be silent and hear from God as HE directs you on the path in which you are to go! Once you are still and silent, listen to the instructions as HE directs you in the path in which you are to go and MOST IMPORTANT...TAKE ACTION. God gives you a vision and it is for an appointed time, but WE MUST TAKE ACTION to bring it to fruition.

WEEK 3 – POWER OF P-M-S STUDY

Are you going before God with any of your endeavors?

PRAISE: I can rejoice in knowing that I took the time to be still and listen as HE was speaking and directing.

MEDITATION: Ask God to reveal **HIS** next steps in your life. Be still and hear from HIM before taking any action.

STUDY: *~Psalms 46:10 ~Be still, and know that I am God; I will be exalted among the nations, I will be exalted in the earth!*

The Power of P-M-S: Praise-Meditation-Study

STEPS

ARE YOU SPENDING ALONE/QUALITY TIME WITH GOD?
WHAT IS HE TELLING YOU TO DO IN THIS SEASON?
Write some steps will you take in bringing them to pass.

_____

_____

_____

_____

_____

_____

_____

_____

_____

_____

_____

WEEK 4

~Jeremiah 1:5~
Before I formed thee in the belly, I knew thee; and before thou camest forth out of the womb
I sanctified thee, and I ordained thee a prophet unto the nations.

One night I attended a doctorate dinner and was asked a burning question. "What is your purpose for conducting your dissertation research?" It was then that I realized that before I was in my mother's womb, I was ordained to do this! As I reflect on my life journeys, I can clearly see the map God was preparing for me.

Now is the time to be true to yourself... Now is the time to re-define your purpose...write it down...Don't let it die! WAKE IT UP...WAKE IT UP...WAKE IT UP!!!

WEEK 4 – POWER OF P-M-S STUDY

What is your destiny?

The Power of P-M-S: Praise-Meditation-Study

PRAISE: There may have been forks in the roads, U-turns, dead-ends, traffic, stop signs, red lights, yellow lights, green lights, caution signs, do not enter signs, sudden stops, and some collisions but nothing was coincidental. IT WAS DESTINY!

MEDITATION: Take some time out and reflect on your calling. Many of you know what it is because it is who you are. Pray to God and ask him to guide you in bringing it to pass.

STUDY: *~Jeremiah 1:5~ Before I formed thee in the belly I knew thee; and before thou camest forth out of the womb. I sanctified thee, and I ordained thee.......*

STEPS

Each and every one of us has a purpose to fulfill. I ask that you wake up the dream that is lying dormant in the pit of your soul. If you can recall your life's journey from the day you were born up until now, reflect on it. Do you see any similarities? Does it define your authentic self?
IS IT YOUR DESTINY?

_____

_____

Alicia Middleton

The Power of P-M-S: Praise-Meditation-Study

WEEK 5
~ 2 Corinthians 3:12 ~
Therefore, since we have such a hope, we are very bold

In 2005, I was called to minister alongside my husband, but there were so many WHAT IFS that entered my mind. I often thought WHAT IF my speech impediment prevents me from being understood, WHAT IF my past worldly lifestyle comes back to haunt me? All those WHAT IFS was a deception to block my blessings.

It is through God's promise of hope that I've gained the experiences and growth despite the WHAT IFS. WHO CARES if everyone knows my WHAT IFS, they do not supersede God's hope!

<u>*WEEK 5 – POWER OF P-M-S STUDY*</u>

Your WHAT IFS is not God's Hope

Alicia Middleton

PRAISE: Thank you, Almighty for that special dose of my God-given uniqueness to move on despite the many WHAT IFS.

MEDITATION: Don't let your life be a life of WHAT IFS. Become bold in the hope of the Lord. Continue praying and asking God to move you towards HIS PURPOSE AND PLAN OVER YOUR LIFE DESPITE THE WHAT IFS!

STUDY: ~ *2 Corinthians 3:12* ~ *Therefore, since we have such a hope, we are very bold*

STEPS

WRITE DOWN SOME THINGS THAT GOD IS
TELLING YOU TO DO BUT
YOU ARE THINKING WHAT IF...

_____

_____

_____

_____

The Power of P-M-S: Praise-Meditation-Study

WEEK 6

~John 8:36~
"Therefore if the Son makes you free, you shall be free indeed.

As I reflect over my life. I battled with anxiety that stemmed from a hidden area of guilt that I had to release. On Dec. 29, 1999, as I was sleeping, I vividly recall hearing my daddy yell, "Rainey, I'm free." As I awakened, I ran from my bedroom towards his room. The house was absolutely dark; the sun had yet to rise, but there was a glow. As I opened his bedroom door, I saw my father lying in his bed…breathless. What should I do for my Daddy? I cried, trying to move his motionless body. There was no response, and I panicked! I began waking my mother and sister as silently as I could to avoid waking our babies. "He's gone," I told them. We called for medical assistance. In a flash, my parents' home was flooded with paramedics and our neighboring family members. Everything was going in slow motion. The paramedics were performing CPR on him. As they were working on him, I watched and said to myself, *Alicia what is wrong with you?* Why didn't you perform CPR? You are trained, you knew what to do. A couple of hours later, he was pronounced dead, and I blamed myself.

As soon as his funeral services were over, I went back home to NYC to live my normal life, so I thought! A year later, my sister had to rush me to the hospital. I suffered a major anxiety attack. I became severely depressed, and I wanted to die but couldn't because I had two little ones. They needed me, and then I remembered...Before I ran to my father on the day he died, I awoke to him yelling Rainey…I'm free in my dream. Now as I reflect on the last Christmas we shared, my dad was so happy. He was singing, dancing and telling stories. It was at that moment that I experienced freedom.

The Power of P-M-S: Praise-Meditation-Study

WEEK 6 – POWER OF P-M-S STUDY
Won't you join me in breaking the chains of bondage?

PRAISE: It is seventeen years later, and I can say that I am free of the guilt of not performing CPR and letting the fond memories of my dad envelope my heart as it gives me peace!

MEDITATION: What guilt, shame or un-forgiveness are you holding on to? Pray and ask God for freedom.

STUDY: ~John 8:36~ "Therefore if the Son makes you free, you shall be free indeed."

STEPS

WHAT IS KEEPING YOU IN BONDAGE?
WRITE THEM DOWN AND PROCLAIM YOUR
FREEDOM THROUGH CHRIST JESUS!

_____

_____

_____

_____

_____

Alicia Middleton

WEEK 7

~*Psalm 139:14*~
I will praise You, for I am fearfully and wonderfully made; Marvelous are Your works, And that my soul knows very well.

So many times, I was ashamed of who I was and what I looked like. In Junior High School, I was denied admission into Music & Arts, Norman Thomas and Murry Bergtraum High Schools. In my freshman and sophomore year of high school, I did not make the cheerleading squad. It was during these times I was told that I lacked leadership qualities, high academic grades, focus, coordination, rhythm, precision, and style. Peers told me I was not cute enough, I could not dance, was too skinny, not shapely enough, knocked knees, too dark and wore coca cola bottle glasses. I was even called vamp, short for vampire because of my crooked, sharp teeth with a big gap in the middle! For years, I thought I was the ugliest, dumbest person in the world.

The Power of P-M-S: Praise-Meditation-Study

WEEK 7 – POWER OF P-M-S STUDY

Write down those things that are holding you back from accepting your inner and outer beauties?

***PRAISE*:** LOOK AT WHERE GOD HAS BROUGHT ME FROM! Today, I rejoice in knowing that I am wonderfully made by God!

MEDITATION: Never let anyone or anything take you off course. Remember you were perfectly made by God! Continue to pray and ask God for strength to endure during your moments of weakness. Although, it may appear to be true, remember that God designed YOU. Build that bond with HIM and let HIM reveal who you are in HIM.

STUDY: ~Psalm 139:14~I will praise You, for I am fearfully and wonderfully made;
Marvelous are Your works, And that my soul knows very well.

STEPS.

Write down those things that are holding you back from accepting your inner and outer them?
Write down ways you can rebuke them.

_____

_____

_____

_____

_____

_____

_____

_____

_____

The Power of P-M-S: Praise-Meditation-Study

WEEK 8

~Jeremiah 30:17~
For I will restore health to you
And heal you of your wounds,' says the LORD.

What is this pain? I could not walk without wanting to fall to the ground. Let me sit for a moment. OH MY GOD, that's painful too. I will try to lie down in my favorite fetal position. I can't do that either the pain was too excruciating. I got on the floor, and that hurt too. Okay, I'll try lying flat on my back; still painful. Let me put my feet up to get a little comfort. Now, I will soak in a hot tub. I couldn't do that either. THERE'S NO RELIEF.

I visited my doctor...he suggested having an X-ray completed. "Mrs. Middleton," he says, "You have osteopenia, the beginning stages of osteoporosis".

"IT CAN'T BE, I'M ONLY 44," I stated. He suggested some blood work and an MRI. The reports show that I have no Vitamin D, curvature of the spine and spots on my spine. My discs are herniated which is impinging the nerve that traveled from my lower back to my toes. He recommends surgery as an option but could not guarantee that I will be healed from pain. He claimed that there's no healing for disc herniation. I will suffer with this condition for my entire life. As a result of this report, I was diagnosed with degenerative disc disease. Another option was therapy as it will enhance my quality of life by providing some comfort. As a result of this condition and therapy, I could not work. What now....my body was in pain but my mind was full of ideas. There was no way I was giving into this condition.

WEEK 8 – POWER OF P-M-S STUDY

Whose report will you believe?

PRAISE: TODAY, I AM WALKING IN MY HEALING......through my WEEKLY SPIRITUAL P-M-S, MY HEALTH IS BEING RESTORED!

The Power of P-M-S: Praise-Meditation-Study

MEDITATION: PRAY FOR YOUR HEALING TODAY! NO MATTER WHAT THE MEDICAL REPORT SAYS BELIEVE IN TOTAL COMPLETE HEALING.

STUDY: *~Jeremiah 30:17~For I will restore health to you And heal you of your wounds,' says the LORD.*

STEPS

WRITE DOWN ALL YOUR ACHES AND PAINS AND MEDICAL REPORTS.

CLAIM HEALING OVER YOUR AILMENTS

_____

_____

_____

_____

_____

_____

_____

_____

Alicia Middleton

WEEK 9

~Proverbs 22:6~
Train up a child in the way he should go,
And when he is old he will not depart from it.

My hardships were not the result of a bad childhood; it was the result of poor judgment and decisions on my part. My parents relocated from Florida in the 50's to escape racism to provide a better quality of life for my sister and I. I am a GPK (grand Preacher's Kid). My grandfather, uncle, and first generation cousins were/are prominent religious leaders. My father was a college student at Columbia College, went to Baptist College Theological School, married my mother and provided for my sister and I. My mother was the backbone of my family, a TRUE VIRTUOUS WOMAN, and my sister was the BEST BIG SISTER anyone could ask for and have. I WAS LOVED UNCONDITIONALLY; some say I was spoiled. Love was in my childhood, and the Christian faith was my foundation. SO WHAT HAPPENED?

The Power of P-M-S: Praise-Meditation-Study

I departed for a moment. Thought the bible was man's way of keeping people in bondage. I joined The Hebrew Israelites where they taught me that a man can have more than one wife and when a woman engages in sexual relations with a man, she is married to that man. As a result, I had children out of wedlock with a man who had another wife leaving me confused and alone. WHAT NOW! Deep within my spirit I still heard a small voice I recognized from my youth.

WEEK 9 – POWER OF P-M-S STUDY

Straying does not mean staying...What foundation are you laying?

PRAISE: As I enter this next phase of life, I am going through a process of healing and deliverance. I am so grateful I had parents who trained me in the way to go.

MEDITATION: Do not get discouraged if you witness some straying. Your child(ren) may stray, but they will BE PLACED RIGHT BACK ON TRACK IF THE FOUNDATION HAS

Alicia Middleton

BEEN LAID! THEY WILL BE SAVED BY YOUR PRAYERS. ASK THE SPIRIT TO GUIDE THEM BACK HOME!

STUDY: *~Proverbs 22:6~Train up a child in the way he should go, And when he is old he will not depart from it.*

STEPS

WHAT FOUNDATION ARE YOU BUILDING FOR YOUR CHILD(REN).
WRITE A PLAN, BE SURE TO INCORPORATE FAMILY WORSHIP
AND/OR MEDITATION

_____

_____

_____

_____

_____

The Power of P-M-S: Praise-Meditation-Study

WEEK 10

~Proverbs 31:10~ Who can find a virtuous wife? For her worth is far above rubies.

As women, we have dreams of the happily ever after like those told in the romantic love stories. We began our childhood by playing house as wives and mommies. Our heart and soul long for love from our little girl days. Therefore, we begin looking for Mr. Right but are often blinded by Mr. Wrong. I can recall the feelings of being in love for the first time. I was the captain of the cheerleading squad, and he was co-captain of the football team. We were the perfect couple of our high school peers. It was so perfect that I was blinded when he would bring her to our games. He introduced me to her as his best friend's girlfriend. He would leave the game with her and his friend to take her home. He also started calling and canceling our dates so that he could take his best friend to visit her. His excuse was his best-friend is new to this country and does not know how to travel. Was I so naive that I did not question to come along nor ask for us to double-date?

Then one day, his niece said to me, "My uncle must really love you because he broke up with her to be with you."

I said, "Broke up with her? Isn't she his best friend's girl?" Then she got quiet and pretended to be joking. I knew deep down she was not and then the pieces started coming together. So I confronted her, and she told me the truth. She said that she had been his girlfriend for over a year now. She went on to say that he did break up with her, but he still visits. I agreed to be a surprise guest at his next visit with her. Deep down I hoped it was not true, but I got the surprise of my life. He was shocked to see me there. At that point, I gave him an ultimatum...ME OR HER...and he chose her.

Years later, I later found out that he married her and they are still married today!

The Power of P-M-S: Praise-Meditation-Study

WEEK 10 – POWER OF P-M-S STUDY

Are you searching for Mr. Right that you are blindsided by Mr. Wrong?

PRAISE: Thankful for being created as a precious jewel and waiting for my husband to find his treasure in me.

MEDITATION: WE AS WOMEN have been conditioned to want to find love. We spend our lives looking for Mr. Right, but in retrospect, our husbands must come find us. We are the precious jewels that must be discovered. Our value is worth far above rubies. Therefore, whoever finds us...finds a treasure...let's take care of our worth, value our worth and wait for God to send true love our way! Through prayer and meditation, HE WILL COME!

STUDY: *~Proverbs 31:10~ Who can find a virtuous wife? For her worth is far above rubies.*

Alicia Middleton

STEPS

WRITE DOWN YOUR JEWELS AND WHEN MR. RIGHT COMES MAKE SURE HE RECOGNIZES THEM AS TREASURES.

_____

_____

_____

_____

_____

_____

_____

_____

_____

_____

_____

The Power of P-M-S: Praise-Meditation-Study

WEEK 11

~1 Peter 3:7~Colossians 3:18, 19
Husbands, likewise, dwell with them with understanding, giving honor to the wife, as to the weaker vessel, and as being heirs together of the grace of life, that your prayers may not be hindered. Wives, submit yourselves unto your own husbands, as it is fit in the Lord. Husbands, love your wives and be not bitter against them.

From the first day we met until now, we've been called into ministry as leaders of the faith. I vividly remember us going before the altar of God twice to receive counseling. We were advised that my husband would be called to minister to His people and the visions would come to me, and he must not fight me on it!

As leaders of the faith, we've been counseled that faith is activated through charity. From the day of my existence in my mother's womb and our existence as husband and wife, I've been commissioned to display unusual acts of charity. It is in my blood, my soul, my spirit, my being. If I deny this calling, I am out of the will of God. Constantly, the bible reminds us of wise men and women of the bible who gave all they had and received favor from the Lord.

As counseled, I began receiving visions to share with my husband, but the devil fights us every step of the way. My husband is a man of FAITH, and I am a woman of LOVE. Although they are two separate gifts, we must deal with one another as heirs to the grace of life.

WEEK 11 – POWER OF P-M-S STUDY

Marriage........sharing the heritage of the grace of life

PRAISE: Giving thanks for the gifts He has given us; independently and collectively!

MEDITATION: I pray that together and independently, we are joined on one accord so that our prayers will not be hindered as we fight the fight of faith in activating our ministry gifts together in unity!

STUDY: ~1 Peter 3:7~Colossians 3:18, 19 - Husbands, likewise, dwell with them with understanding, giving

The Power of P-M-S: Praise-Meditation-Study

honor to the wife, as to the weaker vessel, and as being heirs together of the grace of life, that your prayers may not be hindered. Wives, submit yourselves unto your own husbands, as it is fit in the Lord. Husbands, love [your] wives, and be not bitter against them.

STEPS

WHERE THERE IS DIVISION, THERE IS NO UNITY. Write down some areas in which you can pray with and for your husband.

_____

_____

_____

_____

_____

_____

_____

_____

Alicia Middleton

WEEK 12

~Psalm 37: 23, 24~
The steps of a good man are ordered by the LORD, And He delights in his way.
Though he fall, he shall not be utterly cast down; For the LORD upholds him with His hand.

There is no way that God is trusting me with HIS plan especially after I backslid from my Christian training. God, are you telling me to tell my husband to start a ministry? This is *TOTALLY IMPOSSIBLE* and hard to believe. However, the more I waited, the hotter the fire in my soul became. So I began to write the visions down in my journal. As I am writing, my healing and forgiveness began, and doors began to open. No sooner than I could imagine, I was standing in the courthouse presenting them with the Articles of Incorporation for A New Life Ministry. Soon after, I was given a MAC computer and met with a Time Warner Cable TV producer where I began producing our church services and broadcasting them for residents living in New York City. This was so

The Power of P-M-S: Praise-Meditation-Study

surreal...As I walked down the streets and into stores, people would approach me with, "Aren't you the ministry on TV?"

It did not stop there! My husband and I began traveling to Auburn, NY to conduct services at the Holiday Inn. A few months later, we moved into a building of our own. Within the year, we started an educational ministry for our youth. My congregation and even the Pastor thought I was crazy because we had no qualified personnel to oversee it, but God gave me the directives, and I obeyed His orders.

WEEK 12 - POWER OF P-M-S STUDY

What is my order?

PRAISE: So glad that I followed God's directive when he gave me a burning desire and vision to start a ministry in 2005. Seven years later, I applied for the Doctoral of Educational Administration program at East Stroudsburg University. Not only did I meet the educational requirements, but here I am in

Alicia Middleton

New Mexico directing Quality Improvement and Career Center at San Juan College.

MEDITATION: God please continue to order my steps.

STUDY: *~Psalm 37: 23, 24~The steps of a good man are ordered by the LORD, And He delights in his way. Though he fall, he shall not be utterly cast down; For the LORD upholds him with His hand.*

STEPS

You will never reach your plateau, if you never step out on faith.
Write down a few steps that you will begin to take TODAY!

_____

_____

_____

_____

_____

The Power of P-M-S: Praise-Meditation-Study

WEEK 13
~ (Ephesians 6:11) ~
Put on the whole armor of God that you may be able to stand against the wiles of the devil.

Many people feel that as a woman in the ministry, I reveal too much. In other words, I publicize my personal business creating opportunities for me to be judged and criticized. My response to that is this, I am a woman in the ministry, but I breathe, live, and must survive the same as everyone else. I AM NO DIFFERENT! What sets me apart is my transparency so that others can see how I strive to remain healthy and successful. Please understand that I get attacked just like everyone else. Although it took some time, I have learned to protect myself from the wiles of mankind. My protection comes from my protector. Unfortunately, we cannot stop Satan but God can.

WEEK 13 – POWER OF P-M-S STUDY

Protect Yourself

Alicia Middleton

PRAISE: I am a living testimony! I am not ashamed of the gospel or sharing my life experiences as I journey on the path to my destiny!

MEDITATION: I will continuously seek refuge under your shield as it armors me.

STUDY: *~Ephesians 6:11~* Put on the whole armor of God, that you may be able to stand against the wiles of the devil.

STEPS

The main reason people are unhealthy is because THEY ALLOW THEIR LIFE TO BE CONSUMED WITH PROBLEMS! Don't let the battles in your life become your downfall. REMEMBER WE ARE WINNERS BECAUSE WE CAN DO ALL THINGS IN CHRIST WHO GIVES US STRENGTH! BEGIN MAKING A LIST OF YOUR BATTLES, then turn it over to God. Next, write your success story and let this be a reminder to focus on God's promises and not your problems.

The Power of P-M-S: Praise-Meditation-Study

Alicia Middleton

WEEK 14
~ (Hebrews 13, 1, 2) ~
Let brotherly love continue.
Be not forgetful to entertain strangers: for thereby some have entertained angels unawares.

No matter how fancy or poor someone may appear to be we must treat them with genuine godly love. My momma always told me to never judge a book by its cover. As a youth, I was always teased. I was never the most popular or the best looking. During my middle school years, I failed purposely just to be "down with the in crowd". I got into silly battles to prove that I could fight. However, there was one thing I would never do, and that was teasing. In fact, I would be the one to befriend someone who appeared different or not part of a click. Many of my family and friends could never understand this about me and would try to talk me out of it.

In our meditation scripture, God reminds us to continue our acts and expressions of love, careful not to forget entertaining strangers for they may be angels unaware. What

The Power of P-M-S: Praise-Meditation-Study

would you do if you had the opportunity to entertain Jesus and you did not do it because He did not look the way you expected?

Don't let a smile, frown, fancy clothes, rags, mansion, or shack detain you from displaying the love of God. We do not know what someone may be going through or feeling. Our acts of love may be just what they need to uplift them.

WEEK 14 – POWER OF P-M-S STUDY

What would you do if you had the opportunity to entertain Jesus but did not because He did not look the way you expected?

PRAISE: Thank you for allowing me to display acts of kindness to those in need.

MEDITATION: Direct those who are in need to my path so that I may love on them.

Alicia Middleton

<u>*STUDY:*</u> *~ Hebrews 13:1, 2 ~ Let Brotherly love continue.*

Be not forgetful to entertain strangers: for thereby some have entertained angels unaware.

<u>STEPS</u>

List some ways you can begin displaying acts of kindness towards someone.

_____

_____

_____

_____

_____

_____

_____

_____

_____

_____

_____

The Power of P-M-S: Praise-Meditation-Study

WEEK 15
~ *(Peter 2:9)* ~
But ye are a chosen generation, a royal priesthood, a holy nation, a peculiar people; that ye should shew forth the praises of him who hath called you out of darkness into his marvelous light

Growing up, I've seemed out of place...like I did not belong and was trying to fit in. I grew up in a strict Christian home where I was forbidden to go out to the street jams or chill in the neighborhood park. My peers called me goodie-goodie or nerdy-nerdy. I would often retreat to my room and get lost in my studies or travel to lands of serenity in the books I've read.

During the summer, my parents would send me to West Palm Beach and Callahan, Florida to keep me from staying alone in our New York City apartment while they worked. I was known as Miss Proper or that city girl. I found it difficult to feel at home with my cousins. However, I would witness how involved they were in athletics. At that time, I was

Alicia Middleton

spastic and could not play any of the sports nor dance, but I valued my time in watching them.

When I came back to NYC, I was determined to get involved in high school athletics. My freshmen year, I did not make the track team or the cheerleading squad. I absolutely had no athletic abilities whatsoever, but I was determined to work hard at it. During my freshmen and sophomore year, I would work out with the track team and ran some cross country events where I always came in last place. I joined the boosters and worked on my gymnastic skills. No matter how much I was teased, I was persistent and practiced hard until I was able to do a cartwheel, round-off and split. My junior year, I finally made the squad and went on to become the captain my senior year. I graduated high school with high honors and went to York College where I majored in physical education.

The Power of P-M-S: Praise-Meditation-Study

Embracing my peculiarity!

<u>**PRAISE**</u>*:* Today, I continue to stand apart, but I've learned to accept that I have been chosen in my uniqueness where I will forever let my light shine ever so bright!

<u>**MEDITATION**</u>*:* Lord, help me to embrace my peculiarity and let my light forever shine brightly.

<u>**STUDY**</u>*: ~Peter 2:9~ But ye are a chosen generation, a royal priesthood, a holy nation, a peculiar people; that ye should shew forth the praises of him who hath called you out of darkness into his marvelous light*

Alicia Middleton

STEPS

List the traits that separate you from everyone else and embrace them through the love of God

_____

_____

_____

_____

_____

_____

_____

_____

_____

_____

_____

_____

The Power of P-M-S: Praise-Meditation-Study

WEEK 16

~ *(John 13:34)* ~
*A new commandment I give to you, that you love one another;
as I have loved you, that you also love one another.*

Last night, I had an AWESOME time at East Stroudsburg University's Voices of Triumph Gospel Choir. The Spirit of the Lord was in that place. However, I left with a burden on my heart. During the playing of a worship song, the psalmist began mentioning acts of sin. Someone got up and ran out in tears. I immediately followed, but I could not find them. I WAS HURT!!!

God put this word in my heart. My job is to minister the word of God to all, especially those who are hurting. It is the job of the HOLY SPIRIT to heal and deliver. Jesus left us with this final commandment to love one another as I have loved you. As we look at how Jesus loved, he loved the woman who was caught in the act of adultery...he even loved the one who betrayed him. FOR THERE IS NO SIN THAT IS

Alicia Middleton

GREATER THAN THE OTHER. Jesus said, he who is without sin, cast the first stone.

At this concert, the entire audience should have walked out in tears, but they did not because many knew they were saved by the blood of Jesus. It is unfortunate that many hurting people are unaware of this and may feel that they are not worthy of God's love because they were not taught salvation through LOVE... As a result, they continue to fall into many temptations...some may even take their lives.

WEEK 16 – POWER OF P-M-S STUDY
LOVE SOMEBODY TODAY!

PRAISE: Jesus commanded us that our job is to LOVE....embrace the person and allow God's Spirit to heal and deliver. I just prayed that I had the opportunity to just hug this person, wipe away their tears and let them know that they are loved!

The Power of P-M-S: Praise-Meditation-Study

MEDITATION: I want to have the heart of Jesus and love with the love He has given me!

STUDY: *~ John 13:34~ A new commandment I give to you, that you love one another; as I have loved you, that you also love one another.*

STEPS

Who do you know that is hurting? Make a list and reach out to them with a loving gesture.

_____

_____

_____

_____

_____

_____

_____

Alicia Middleton

WEEK 17

~ (Matthew 18:15-17) ~
Moreover if your brother sins against you, go and tell him his fault between you and him alone. If he hears you, you have gained your brother. But if he will not hear, take with you one or two more, that 'by the mouth of two or three witnesses every word may be established.'
And if he refuses to hear them, tell it to the church. But if he refuses even to hear the church, let him be to you like a heathen and a tax collector.

I will never forget when I started assessing those whom I considered my personal and intimate friends. I began to take notice of what we brought into each other's lives. As a Grand PK (grand-daughter of a Reverend) who grew into becoming the wife of a Pastor and a minister of the gospel myself. My private circle was very important and dear to me. I began noticing that everyone who I thought was my friend...actually were not! In fact, as I achieved for greater things, the harder they pulled me away from that path. Each and every time they were in my presence, they were plotting on their next scam of getting over just to get ahead. Not realizing they were hurting themselves and others. You thought they were in the faith

The Power of P-M-S: Praise-Meditation-Study

walking with you, but their actions said something else. What made it even sadder is that they were so sick with this addiction that they did not know they were hurting others.

When you try to speak to them, they are in denial and claim it is you. You see their desperation and your heart fills up with compassion, but they mistake this gesture as weakness and continue with attempting to entangle you in their web of deceit.

God says, if two or more shall agree on earth as touching anything that they shall ask, it shall be done. I am ready for the Favor of God, and I willingly accept the friendship of those who are in agreement.

WEEK 17 – POWER OF P-M-S STUDY
YOU HAVE OFFENDED ME!

PRAISE: Through these experiences, I have learned to call upon His word for advice. We must learn to follow His principles and not let our emotions get the best of us. As a child of God, we must adhere to these steps:

Alicia Middleton

MEDITATION: Many people want to avoid drama in their lives. However, God left us a blueprint. Ask Him to guide you in dealing with those who offend you!

STUDY: ~Matthew 18: 15 -17 ~ *"Moreover if your brother sins against you, go and tell him his fault between you and him alone. If he hears you, you have gained your brother. But if he will not hear, take with you one or two more, that 'by the mouth of two or three witnesses every word may be established. And if he refuses to hear them, tell it to the church. But if he refuses even to hear the church, let him be to you like a heathen and a tax collector"*

STEPS IN DEALING WITH OFFENSE

1. Go to them privately and tell them their offense against you. If they listen, you have gained them back.
2. If not, take one or two others so that every word may be established.
3. If they offend you again, tell it unto the church (a group of advisors not gossipers)
4. If they offend you again use caution when proceeding with this friendship.

What offense are you dealing with? How will you use the above steps in bringing peace?

The Power of P-M-S: Praise-Meditation-Study

WEEK 18

~ (Corinthians 13: 4-8) ~

Love is patient, love is kind and is not jealous; love does not brag and is not arrogant, does not act unbecomingly; it does not seek its own, is not provoked, does not take into account a wrong suffered, does not rejoice in unrighteousness, but rejoices with the truth; bears all things, believes all things, hopes all things, endures all things. LOVE NEVER FAILS!

Puppy love...oh the feeling, the palpitations of your heart beating, the tingling of your skin and the mushy feeling in your tummy. We all want to experience the grandeur of being in love. The romantic dinners, the walks in the parks, the holding of hands and the glow in your eyes. WHAT A FEELING!

Then reality hits...time has passed, and the true person is revealed. What happened to the person you fell in love with? The lies and deceit. The road is now replaced with thoughts of what was instead of accepting what is. We begin making excuses in hopes of the flame returning.

What is Godly love? God has designed how love should be expressed and displayed.

WEEK 18 – POWER OF P-M-S STUDY

The Power of P-M-S: Praise-Meditation-Study

FAIRY TALE LOVE OR A GODLY LOVE RELATIONSHIP

PRAISE: We must begin expressing and accepting a Godly love. It's time to evaluate our relationships.

MEDITATION: Are we giving and accepting a FAIRY TALE MAKE BELIEVE LOVE OR DISPLAYING THE ATTRIBUTES OF A GODLY LOVE RELATIONSHIP?

STUDY: *~Corinthians 13:4-8 ~ Love is patient, love is kind and is not jealous; love does not brag and is not arrogant, does not act unbecomingly; it does not seek its own, is not provoked, does not take into account a wrong suffered, does not rejoice in unrighteousness, but rejoices with the truth; bears all things, believes all things, hopes all things, endures all things. LOVE NEVER FAILS!*

STEPS

Make a list of the characteristics displayed in your relationship as defined in
Corinthians 13: 4-8, if these characteristics are not dominant, it's time to examine your relationship.

Alicia Middleton

The Power of P-M-S: Praise-Meditation-Study

<u>WEEK 19</u>

~ (Isaiah 61:3) ~
To console those who mourn in Zion, to give them beauty for ashes,
The oil of joy for mourning, the garment of praise for the spirit of heaviness;
That they may be called trees of righteousness,
The planting of the LORD, that He may be glorified.

Moving to Pennsylvania separated me from family and friends. The first couple of months, I knew no one. Not to mention I was just diagnosed with a painful degenerative disc disease. This was hard as my days were wrecked in pain. I could not walk and had to crawl up the stairs to go into my bedroom. The therapy and pain medication were not working. It just left me in a stupor whenever I took them.

My husband had to stay in New York City to work, leaving me with a heaviness in my spirit. Why did I move miles away from my family and friends? There was no one I could call for help. I woke up at six am and to take my children to the bus stop and come home to take my medication. I slept until two pm to awake to pick them up again. I try to study for two hours and then take my meds again to repeat this cycle.

Alicia Middleton

I had just enrolled in this master program. How will I complete it in such pain? I am grateful that I can take my courses online, but it is so hard. I am able to prop myself in bed for a few hours but for how long. Please, God give me strength I pray.

On Sundays, we traveled three hours to the church my husband, Pastored. He takes the seat out in the back of the van so I can lie down flat for the ride. When we arrived at the church, I prepared refreshments for the congregation and conducted Praise & Worship...all the while I'm bent over and can barely walk.

WEEK 19 – POWER OF P-M-S STUDY

Dancing in the Rain!

PRAISE: No matter how I feel, I am going to PRAISE and in that moment, there's no pain. For the spirit of heaviness, I WILL PUT ON A GARMENT OF PRAISE! It is then that I live my sorrow at the altar and turn it over to God!

MEDITATION: What are you battling with today? Do you feel alone? Do you feel unloved? There will be times in your life when you have to encourage yourself in the Lord. You are never

The Power of P-M-S: Praise-Meditation-Study

alone...God wants to show you His love. It is time to bond with God. He longs and desires to have a personal, intimate relationship with You and You Alone!

<u>STUDY:</u> ~ (Isaiah 61:3) ~To console those who mourn in Zion, To give them beauty for ashes, The oil of joy for mourning, The garment of praise for the spirit of heaviness;

That they may be called trees of righteousness, the planting of the LORD,

that He may be glorified.

Alicia Middleton

STEPS

List the storms that you are passing through so you can begin to dance through them.

_____

_____

_____

_____

_____

_____

_____

_____

_____

_____

_____

_____

The Power of P-M-S: Praise-Meditation-Study

WEEK 20

~ (Proverbs 15:22) ~
Without counsel, plans go awry, But in the multitude of counselors they are established.

As I reflect on the many directions, I took in life I attribute many of my decisions based upon counsel. I'll never forget the beginning stages of my career. For the first few years, I was single with no children and had no major responsibilities. Teaching became my life. At that time, I was working for two great administrators. One who was young and full of vision and the other who had years of teaching and administrative experiences who insisted that I apply for a teaching scholarship at Hunter College.

As I entered my thirties, I began considering parenting and marriage. I wanted a family of my own before I became too old to do so. At the age of twenty-eight, I became pregnant, but that pregnancy ended in a stillborn birth. Immediately after delivery, I went back to teaching full-time. Two years later, I became pregnant again. This time, it was diagnosed as high risk.

Alicia Middleton

I was advised by my doctors to go on complete bed rest. However, I chose to continue working but vowed to take it easy.

Toward the end of that pregnancy, the young administrator entered my classroom with another teacher to inform me that she was not pleased with my loss of stamina and energy. I was crushed, but I realized she was right. I knew that this administrator was very demanding due to her focus on starting a new school and she expected her staff to be totally committed to teaching. In the beginning of my career, teaching was my only priority. However, my life had new dimensions whereas teaching was not my sole priority anymore. At that point, I had to choose what was best for this administrator, the school, the students and myself. As a result, I chose motherhood and ended my teaching career.

I transferred back into the main office working for an amazing principal in payroll processing. This administrator would constantly remind me that working in the office was

The Power of P-M-S: Praise-Meditation-Study

momentarily and that soon I would come from behind that desk.

WEEK 20 – POWER OF P-M-S STUDY

Receiving Wise Counsel

PRAISE: My life is following its course based on wise counseling.

MEDITATION: Lead me to the ones who guides me in the right direction.

STUDY: *~Proverbs 15:22 ~ Without counsel, plans go awry, But in the multitude of counselors they are established.*

STEPS

What decisions are you making for your life? Are you receiving wise spiritual, professional, and personal counseling? We must be extremely careful in whom we seek and receive counseling in deciding the right steps to take in our lives. Begin to evaluate and list those whom you will seek counsel from.

Alicia Middleton

The Power of P-M-S: Praise-Meditation-Study

WEEK 21

~ (Matthew 6:10) ~
Your kingdom come. Your will be done. On earth as it is in heaven.

As I reflect over the accomplishments of this past year, I think of this scripture, "Your kingdom come, your will be done ON EARTH AS IT IS IN HEAVEN". Many people believe heaven is in the sky and will be obtained when we die if we live right and accept Jesus here on earth.

What is the meaning of this? As for me, I want to make my life meaningful while on earth. I want people to speak well of me so that I can present myself acceptable before God. I want to surround myself with those of like minds who will live their life here on earth with a kingdom mindset.

During this past year, I've met new friends whom I will continue building satisfying relationships with, and I've had to let go of those who were not pleasing. Life is full of choices that we must make. If we pray, build a relationship with God and let him direct us toward the path in which we should go, we can achieve the desires of our hearts here on earth so that we can present ourselves before God with delight.

WEEK 21 – POWER OF P-M-S STUDY

My Kingdom Here on Earth!

PRAISE: We have the power to reach our destination when we build a satisfying relationship with God.

MEDITATION: Guide me in building my kingdom.

STUDY: ~ Matthew 6:10 ~ Your kingdom come. Your will be done. On earth as it is in heaven.

The Power of P-M-S: Praise-Meditation-Study

STEPS

Do not be dismayed if you have to end or cut off something that is not favorable for you. Make wise choices that will enable you to stay on your God ordained path here on earth. List the steps in which you will go as you begin building your kingdom. Be sure to include the unfavorable things in your life.

_____

_____

_____

_____

_____

_____

_____

_____

_____

WEEK 22
~ (2 Peter 1:7 (NIV)) ~
And to godliness, mutual affection and to mutual affection, love

As I awake on this cold, snowy day, my mind drifts back to the days of my youth. Oh, what great memories of my mother's hot oatmeal seasoned just right with sugar, butter, and raisins. My father coming in from the cold, after a long night of driving the bus, picking me up, to give me a big Papa Bear hug and my sister whom I shared a room with. We would lie in our twin beds under the covers watching Cooley High, Claudine, Good Times, Welcome Back Kotter and so many shows on days like this.

Growing up meant a lot of maturing, but I would always retreat to my comfort zone of being a little girl. Snuggling in a fetal position with my pillow and my childhood habit (those who know me well, knows what this is). As a woman, I never lost the ability to find my comfort zone and get lost in the affections of my youth. Affection for me is

The Power of P-M-S: Praise-Meditation-Study

snuggling, cuddling, hugging. Watching old movies all bundled up in the covers or reading a book while drinking hot apple cider or just simply daydreaming while in a pair of warm, comfy PJ's.

WEEK 22 – POWER OF P-M-S STUDY

We were designed to be affectionate

PRAISE: Affection and being affectionate strengthens me!

MEDITATION: Lead me to the innermost realm of worship where my soul rejoices.

STUDY: ~ *(2 Peter 1:7 (NIV)) ~And to godliness, mutual affection and to mutual affection, love*

Alicia Middleton

STEPS

What are the affections of your heart that brings you to your comfort zone? We were created to receive and give affection. So if you want to retreat to a place that is buried within your heart. Peel away the layers and let your affections provide you with comfort.

_____

_____

_____

_____

_____

_____

_____

_____

The Power of P-M-S: Praise-Meditation-Study

WEEK 23

~ (Proverbs 27:9) ~
Ointment and perfume delight the heart and the sweetness of a man's friend gives delight by hearty counsel.

I'll never forget how I met her. I was in my second year with the NYC Department of Education, and her daughter was my student. I was young, full of innovation and connected with all of my students. Many veteran teachers gave me a hard time implementing new ideas. This particular school had a basketball team, and I wanted to start a cheerleading squad. I would receive comments such as, "Cheerleaders are not necessary," "Why do girls have to cheer for the boys," "You are degrading our girls by making them wear skirts," "They will distract the boys" and the list goes on and on!

Being young and new to this profession, I did not have the gift of "Politics" and often felt bullied by veteran teachers, but someone came to my rescue. She was a well-known parent

Alicia Middleton

and the director of Women's Services at our local hospital. She took me under her wing. Not only did we have a cheerleading squad at the school, but we had a dance team and a flag team that marched with our band. We performed all over New York City at many public events. This woman rallied up the parents, the community and came to my defense so I would not stand alone. She put the power in my wings to soar. I can still hear her counsel resounding in my head, "Girl you better stand up and not let these folks scare you. You have a voice. I want you to roar like a lion, and to this day, I can't shut up!

WEEK 23 – POWER OF P-M-S STUDY
True Friendship

PRAISE: Her friendship, her counsel and her belief in me has supported and encouraged me as an educator but more in recognizing the value of true friendships.

The Power of P-M-S: Praise-Meditation-Study

MEDITATION: Lead me to true friendship where together we are strong, walking in our path to our GOD ORDAINED PURPOSE!

STUDY: ~ *Proverbs 27:9* ~ *Ointment and perfume delight the heart, and the sweetness of a man's friend gives delight by hearty counsel.*

STEPS

Your friendship(s) should be as sweet smelling perfume which delights your heart. If you are experiencing a friendship that is vexing your spirit, list the things that are affecting you and re-evaluate the makings of true friendships.

_____

_____

_____

_____

_____

Alicia Middleton

The Power of P-M-S: Praise-Meditation-Study

WEEK 24

~ (Proverbs 3: 5, 6) ~
Trust in the LORD with all your heart, and lean not on your own understanding;
In all your ways acknowledge Him, And He shall direct your paths....

WHAT ARE YOU THANKFUL FOR!

I mean really, what are you thankful for? Oftentimes, we focus on the woulda, shoulda, coulda's of life. Never realizing that for everything there is a reason, season, purpose, and time.

This morning, I woke up with this waking thought. I always blamed myself and others for not pursuing my teaching scholarship in the 90's. My ifs were depressing me. When I left this career behind me, I transferred to JHS 117 where I met a good friend. Unbeknownst to me, she was my future sister-in-law. Yes, God had orchestrated this move so that I could cross paths with my husband!

When God says move, you better get to that destination and wait for Him to give you further instructions. He will not give us the entire vision at once. If he did, we would not be able to handle it. We just have to get there! Move when He says move and be still when He says this is not the time. If I would have followed what I thought was my path, I would not be where I am today!

WEEK 24 – POWER OF P-M-S STUDY
WHAT ARE YOU THANKFUL FOR!

PRAISE: Thanking you for staying on the path and not giving up when things did not appear as I wanted.

MEDITATION: Lord teach me to trust in your plan and not get lost in what I may believe to be my plan.

STUDY: ~ *Proverbs 3: 5, 6 ~Trust in the LORD with all your heart, and lean not on your own understanding; In all your ways acknowledge Him, And He shall direct your paths....*

The Power of P-M-S: Praise-Meditation-Study

STEPS

We must learn to Trust wholeheartedly in the Lord with all of our heart...not some with bits and pieces here and there. But all and not lean on our own understanding...we may not see it, but we must believe it, and HE WILL DIRECT OUR PATH! List some things that may not be as you plan, but you will trust in God and follow the path that is opening for you to walk in!

_____

_____

_____

_____

_____

_____

_____

_____

Alicia Middleton

WEEK 25

~ *(James 1:7)* ~
Every good gift and every perfect gift is from above and comes down from the Father of lights, with whom there is no variation or shadow of turning.

Today, I celebrate LIFE...the day that God breathed into my nostrils. I celebrate the Father, The Son, and The Holy Ghost. I celebrate my husband, son, daughter, mother, sister, nephews, nieces, aunts, uncles and cousins. I celebrate my friends, colleagues, and associates. I celebrate those who've entered my life for a reason, season or a lifetime.

WEEK 25 – POWER OF P-M-S STUDY

It's time to celebrate!

PRAISE: Today, I celebrate because God is just that great!

MEDITATION: Put on some good music or do something that makes you feel good!

STUDY: ~James 1:17~ *Every good gift and every perfect gift is from above, and comes down from the Father of*

The Power of P-M-S: Praise-Meditation-Study

lights, with whom there is no variation or shadow of turning

STEPS

List everything that you are thankful for, just because God is that Good!

_____

_____

_____

_____

_____

_____

_____

_____

Alicia Middleton

WEEK 26

~ *(Matthews 25:40)* ~
'Truly I tell you, whatever you did for one of the least of these brothers and sisters of mine, you did for me.

It's time to reevaluate ourselves in how we treat others. If Jesus was your friend, spouse, colleague, etc. how would you treat Him? In the passage above, Jesus explains that whatever... you do for brothers and sisters of mine, you did for me. Would you speak to Jesus with your ego, would you tell Him like it is because that's just who you are or would you question HIS motive of dying on the cross because you think He had a hidden agenda and wanted something from you for HIS benefit. Better yet would you offend Him in order to express how you feel!

Unfortunately, the answer for most of us is YES; we would put Him back on that cross like what was done years ago. We have to stop making excuses such as:

- I'm a work in process
- This is who I am

The Power of P-M-S: Praise-Meditation-Study

- I have a wall up and will only exhibit this with whom I choose
- I won't exhibit this with just anyone until they prove they are worthy
- Once they take me there, I will go there
- This is how I speak or act (I mean no harm) and/or
- You feel that telling them the truth with harshness is an acceptable form of communication

WEEK 26 – POWER OF P-M-S STUDY
MISTREATMENT IS WRONG!

PRAISE: Thank you for teaching me to stop making excuses when I display other attributes that are not of the spirit.

MEDITATION: Teach me O Lord the ways of treating others as Christ treats me

STUDY: ~ *(Matthews 25:40)* ~ *'Truly I tell you, whatever you did for one of the least of these brothers and sisters of mine, you did for me.*

Alicia Middleton

STEPS

We must accept responsibility by taking the first step to take time to think before reacting or speaking. We must learn to humble ourselves and leave our ego behind.

List some of your behaviors that can be egotistical and decide to stop making excuses for them. This will help you to overcome them.

_____

_____

_____

_____

_____

_____

_____

The Power of P-M-S: Praise-Meditation-Study

WEEK 27
~ (Psalm 51:10) ~
Create in me a clean heart, O God, And renew a steadfast spirit within me.

God is not pleased with chaos in ministry. It's time to stop this foolishness in ministry with our brethren. The lying, hate, arrogance, abuse, ego, jealousy, conceit, deceit, insecurity, backbiting, selfishness, unmannerly, uncivil, standoffish, impolite, rude, assertive ways just to get things done while hurting others are not acceptable in Christian living. There's a saying that hurt people will hurt people.

IT'S TIME TO HEAL AND BE DELIVERED FROM THESE UNGODLY AND UN-CHRIST LIKE WAYS. There's no excuse! If you've been hurt and want to heal, you must come from behind this mess. Confess and realize that this is unacceptable behavior.

WEEK 27 – POWER OF P-M-S STUDY

GOD CANNOT BLESS MESS!

PRAISE: I am thankful for God's blessings!

Alicia Middleton

MEDITATION: It's time for renewal! Let's go before God and asked to be healed from the pain that catapults unacceptable behaviors. Allow His peace to restore and create a pure heart and renew a steadfast spirit within!

STUDY: ~ ***Psalm 51:10** ~Create in me a clean heart, O God, And renew a steadfast spirit within me.*

STEPS

It's time to bare ourselves and rid ourselves of unwanted behaviors that are poisoning the temple of God which ignites toxins in ministry and within ourselves. List ways that are not Christ-like and focus on removing them from your life forever!

_____

_____

_____

_____

_____

The Power of P-M-S: Praise-Meditation-Study

WEEK 28
~ (Galatians 5: 16, 17)~
I say then: Walk in the Spirit, and you shall not fulfill the lust of the flesh.
For the flesh lusts against the Spirit, and the Spirit against the flesh; and these are contrary to one another, so that you do not do the things that you wish.

THANKING GOD FOR POSITIONING ME.

I've been in the secular world and dealt with corporate behaviors and mannerisms for almost thirty years...

PROUD TO SAY, I am in a position where I can choose what acceptable behavior is and what is not, what environments to work in and where not to work. I no longer have to accept the behaviors of those who can't maintain self-control, arrogance, and/or egotistical behaviors as an excuse for getting business done. I've had the pleasure of working with those who can get the business done by manifesting the fruits of the spirit in any environment and it is such a pleasant, healthy experience WHERE EVERYONE'S A WINNER!

The Power of P-M-S: Praise-Meditation-Study

My passion in my GOD ORDAINED DESTINY of being a minister and administrator is striving to ensure that I exhibit the Fruits of the Spirit at all times and not be consumed with those who exhibit the fruits of the flesh and if I, myself, fall short...I will accept responsibility for my actions, not make up excuses as a cover up and begin making conscious efforts to stay aligned! This is how we will win the war of Spirit vs. Flesh!

WEEK 28 – POWER OF P-M-S STUDY
FLESH PLEASE SIT DOWN!

PRAISE: Building the kingdom here on earth will create HEALTHY RELATIONSHIPS which creates HEALTHY WORKING ENVIRONMENTS which creates HEALTHY COMMUNITIES THUS BUILDING THE KINGDOM OF GOD!

MEDITATION: Lord help me to identify when I am operating in the flesh and not in the spirit!

Alicia Middleton

<u>STUDY:</u> ~ *(Galatians 5: 16, 17)* ~*I say then: Walk in the Spirit, and you shall not fulfill the lust of the flesh. For the flesh lusts against the Spirit, and the Spirit against the flesh; and these are contrary to one another, so that you do not do the things that you wish.*

<u>*STEPS*</u>

What are some attributes that you might be battling between the spirit and the flesh? Make a list and begin turning the flesh over to the spirit of God.

_____

_____

_____

_____

_____

_____

The Power of P-M-S: Praise-Meditation-Study

WEEK 29

~ (Matthew 10:11-13) ~
Now whatever city or town you enter, inquire who in it is worthy, and stay there till you go out. And when you go into a household, greet it. If the household is worthy, let your peace come upon it. But if it is not worthy, let your peace return to you."

Lately, I've been writing about exhibiting love, displaying the fruits of the spirit, but how do we love when someone does not know how to accept or respect the love you offer. The more we display the fruits of the spirit, the more they display the fruits of the flesh creating an unhealthy, unbalanced state of being for you.

People are hurting, and many want the love we offer but can't or don't know how to receive it, through no fault of our own. They see us as the culprit with some ulterior motive. So what do we do? We love them spiritually through prayer.

Oftentimes, we try to do the job of the Holy Spirit by forcing ourselves on them. By doing this, we may create resentment and hurt on both parties. We must back away and give them space. By doing so does not mean doing so with contentious behavior or arrogance. In fact, we don't have to tell them we're moving on because of their behavior. Just simply back off slowly, but continue reminding them we are there whenever they need us.

WEEK 29 – POWER OF P-M-S STUDY
ALLOWING ROOM FOR GROWTH

PRAISE: Thank you Holy Spirit for entering the hearts of our loved ones.

MEDITATION: WE prayerfully pray for a blessing upon our loved ones by keeping the love and peace in our hearts and praying for the deliverance of our loved ones.

STUDY: *~Matthew 10:11-13~Now whatever city or town you enter, inquire who in it is worthy, and stay there till you go out. And when you go into a household, greet it. If the*

The Power of P-M-S: Praise-Meditation-Study

household is worthy, let your peace come upon it. But if it is not worthy, let your peace return to you."

STEPS

We must learn not to force ourselves upon anyone. Analyze those who may need space but who you will prayerfully keep in your heart.

_____

_____

_____

_____

_____

_____

_____

_____

Alicia Middleton

WEEK 30

~ (Matthew 19:4-6) ~
"Have you not read that He who created them from the beginning MADE THEM MALE AND FEMALE, and said, 'FOR THIS REASON A MAN SHALL LEAVE HIS FATHER AND MOTHER AND BE JOINED TO HIS WIFE, AND THE TWO SHALL BECOME ONE FLESH'? So they are no longer two, but one flesh. What therefore God has joined together, let no man separate."

Being labeled disabled has truly haunted me in my marriage. Our marriage began with us both being financially secure in our careers. As a result, we purchased and built our dream home in Pennsylvania. Six months later, I had to stop working due to my health. What was I going to do? I had acquired the years to retire but not the age. I had the option to apply for an early disability retirement, but it would take years to reach a settlement. As a result, we were without income and our finances suffered tremendously. We were threatening to lose all that we worked hard for. I felt responsible because my health diagnosis and inability to work caused my husband's credit and finances to suffer as well. During this time, I was put

The Power of P-M-S: Praise-Meditation-Study

in a position to determine what finances needed to be paid for our family's survival which resulted in credit card bills not being paid. The income we had coming in only afforded us to take care of our living expenses such as shelter expenses. I took responsibility and blame for it, not realizing that this was a test of our vows. When we went before God and made our vows to be one, during the good and bad in sickness and health forsaking all others until death do us part, it meant exactly that!

WEEK 30 – POWER OF P-M-S STUDY
WORKING AS ONE FLESH WITH MY SPOUSE

PRAISE: Thank you for the gift of unity as God ordained marriage as the first ministry!

MEDITATION: I pray that together and independently, we are joined on one accord so that our prayers will not be hindered as we fight the fight of faith through the good and bad times, together as one!

STUDY: ~ *(Matthew 19:4-6)* ~"Have you not read that He who created them from the beginning MADE THEM MALE AND FEMALE, and said, 'FOR THIS REASON A MAN SHALL LEAVE HIS FATHER AND MOTHER AND BE JOINED TO HIS WIFE, AND THE TWO SHALL BECOME ONE FLESH'? "So they are no longer two, but one flesh. What therefore God has joined together, let no man separate."

STEPS

Pray with your spouse and make a list of ways that you both can support one another through it all!

_____

_____

_____

_____

_____

_____

_____

The Power of P-M-S: Praise-Meditation-Study

WEEK 31

~ (Hebrews 11:1) ~
Now faith is the substance of things hoped for, the evidence of things not seen.

Having one of those days when I don't want to get up out of bed. For the past few weeks, my life has been haywire. Last week, I had to cancel the community outreach bible sharing because the location did not work out, my nephew is leaving, I'm struggling to raise funds to send my son abroad to study, and I can't think of a topic for my seminar term paper.

God has never failed me yet. When it appeared that I had fallen or was momentarily stuck; He steps in....right on time...to pick me up. Today is the day that I will activate my faith!

WEEK 31 – POWER OF P-M-S STUDY

FAITH IT UNTIL I MAKE IT!

PRAISE: Thank you for refueling me!

Alicia Middleton

MEDITATION: Lord, I feel depleted but will rely on your strength to uplift me!

STUDY: ~ *(Hebrews 11:1)* ~ *Now faith is the substance of things hoped for, the evidence of things not seen.*

STEPS

Stop whatever you are doing and refuel your energy.

List ways that may give you energy when you are feeling zapped!

_____

_____

_____

_____

_____

_____

_____

The Power of P-M-S: Praise-Meditation-Study

WEEK 32

~ (Romans 12:2) ~
Do not be conformed to this world, but be transformed by the renewing of your mind, that you may prove what is that good and acceptable and perfect will of God.

Being a minister and working in public education where society separates church from state and does not allow God in schools is clearly a misrepresentation when they allow me in schools. I may not be able to preach the word, but I can surely teach through my actions. This is the essence of who I am.

I refuse to be conformed to this world. When you see me, you see Christ. I make it a point to exemplify him in all I do! So when asked why is it that I'm so inspirational, motivational and empowering, I let it be known that I am a minister, co-pastor, but more importantly A WOMAN OF GOD! I do not allow the dysfunctions of the world to infect me. I seek deliverance by renewing my mind daily through The Power of P-M-S as I press forward towards His destination in my life!

WEEK 32 – POWER OF P-M-S STUDY

I AM WHO I AM BECAUSE OF WHOSE I AM!

PRAISE: Lord, thank you for placing where I can represent you in not just words but by my deeds!

MEDITATION: Give me strength and show me how to represent You in all I do, especially where they impose separation from church and state!

STUDY: ~ *Romans 12:2 ~ Do not be conformed to this world, but be transformed by the renewing of your mind, that you may prove what is that good and acceptable and perfect will of God.*

STEPS

Lead me to righteousness in all that I do, wherever I am!

Make a list of how you can exemplify Christ in arenas that tries to separate church and state

The Power of P-M-S: Praise-Meditation-Study

Alicia Middleton

WEEK 33
~ (1 Corinthians 14:40) ~
Let all things be done decently and in order.

I woke up early this morning with the message, "It's time to GET your life in order for the works I have planned for you." So I organized binders and categorized them according to the works that I've been assigned to do. Such as:

- The Power of P-M-S devotions
- Doctoral Coursework
- Dissertation Research Articles
- Career Development
- Sistah Chat Talk Radio Show
- Monroe County Image Awards

I've set my email and calendars to be stored and sent to my phone. I will check my calendar's agenda every morning to view my daily, weekly, and monthly events to ensure I remain task focused.

The Power of P-M-S: Praise-Meditation-Study

It may appear that I'm doing a lot, but some of the works are to be done today, and others are for the future. These binders are filled with loose leaf paper so as God gives me the direction, I will write, store, and use in its proper timing.

WEEK 33– POWER OF P-M-S STUDY
PRIORITIZE…GET YOUR LIFE IN ORDER!

PRAISE: So thankful for the revelation of prioritizing and setting up systems in place that will keep me focused and on track of accomplishing tasks given for me to complete.

MEDITATION: Lead Me and organize me as I plan my next strategic move.

STUDY: *~1 Corinthians 14:40~ Let all things be done decently and in order.*

Alicia Middleton

STEPS

Set up a system that will work for you as this is your time to get your life in order!

_____

_____

_____

_____

_____

_____

_____

_____

_____

_____

_____

The Power of P-M-S: Praise-Meditation-Study

WEEK 34
~ (2 Corinthians 3:18) ~
As the spirit of the Lord works within us, we become more and more like Him.

I have grown sensitive to things that are not of the spirit. My soul picks up and gets hurt easily whenever there's a tone of arrogance or harshness in speech and action. I will go out of my way for anyone as it reflects Christ that dwells within me. Yes, I am a Christian-straight out of my mother's womb, but I love sharing all forms of spirituality just as long as mine is respected as I am A Woman of the Word of God.

I do not like senseless babble or debate of mistreatment on how we should treat one another. At this stage of life, I choose to bond with those of like minds and actions. I refuse to be bullied and do not like condescending behaviors or attitudes. I am very patient and understand that most people act this way because of their own insecurities or they have been trained to be this way because it appears to show strength. However, I will not let it infect me or allow me to feel uncomfortable or degraded. I am not perfect and will never confess that I am, but I do strive to His perfection at all times. I will not get caught up in the imperfections of this world or think that everything must be perfect as these are lessons I must learn as I continue to receive God's blessing to keep on pressing.

My life is a journey where I am learning something new every step of the way. Therefore, I refuse to accept ultimatums, threats, or demands. If there's a need for anything I will do my best to fulfill it as God directs me. All things work for good for those who love the Lord. Therefore, all things that I do are done to fulfill my purpose, plan, and passion.

WEEK 34– POWER OF P-M-S STUDY

Believing the BEST in all things!

PRAISE: Thank you for allowing me to SEE THE BEST, THINK THE BEST AND BELIEVE THE BEST!

MEDITATION: Make each of my day's positive, creative, fun, and loving memories that I can forever treasure.

The Power of P-M-S: Praise-Meditation-Study

STUDY: ~ *(2 Corinthians 3:18)* ~*As the spirit of the Lord works within us, we become more and more like Him.*

STEPS

Write off those things that are trying to infiltrate you into a world of confusion.

_____

_____

_____

_____

_____

_____

_____

Alicia Middleton

WEEK 35

~ (Jeremiah 29:11) ~
For I know the plans I have for you!

This week I received a C in my conflict resolution class. The first C I ever received in my history of graduate and postgraduate schooling. I had to write a research term paper three times to no avail. I was told that it's amazing that I made it this far in my education without a professor telling me how bad my writing is. I was asked if English was my second language because I do things consistently wrong that I must believe they are right. To top it off, I was told that I probably wouldn't make it through the dissertation process which is the writing and the oral defense.

Ouch...that really hurt and I cried for days. Every emotion of defeat I felt tried to creep within me. I accepted those feelings and allowed myself to mourn. However, I would not remain there nor be defeated. This experience is enlightening as I am seeing God's set up in this. The lower you

The Power of P-M-S: Praise-Meditation-Study

go, the higher you will propel. So while you are in your lows, the key is to allow yourself to express and feel your emotions for a moment, but you must not remain there!

WEEK 35 – POWER OF P-M-S STUDY
GOD IS PROPELLING YOU!

PRAISE: I thank You for your plans that will prosper me by giving me hope in my future.

MEDITATION: I will listen to the words of God and keep His words continually in my mouth!

STUDY: ~*Jeremiah 29:11* ~ **For I know the plans I have for you!**

Alicia Middleton

STEPS

Write down the plans that God has given you as a constant reminder of what He has in store for you!

___
___
___
___
___
___
___
___
___
___
___
___
___

The Power of P-M-S: Praise-Meditation-Study

WEEK 36
~ (Psalms 30:5) ~
For his anger endureth but a moment, in his favour is life: weeping may endure for a night, but joy cometh in the morning

I wish I could write all happy thoughts, but unfortunately, not all posts are going to be that way. We must remember that as we are being set up to propel high, the momentum is generated by how low you go. Like a sling shot, if we want our object to soar high, we must bring it down low. This is the general rule of positioning!

Last night, I had to walk out of class very angry. Lately, I've been having issues with a professor. In a recent meeting, she gave me little hope of success. Last night, when I walked into our classroom, I was overwhelmed with emotion as the memory of our meeting flooded my mind, and I could not control the tears. During our dinner break, I was so overwhelmed that I could not speak with students. However, they were conversing with one another as I listened. Come to find out, there's another student who received a C also. In her meeting, the professor did not speak harshly with her about her personal attributes but critiqued her on ways of improving her literature review. Now listen to this, she asked the student how long it will take her to make revisions and gave her a deadline date of June 30th. She did not allow me this extended option but gave me an earlier deadline of June 10th.

I could not contain my emotions. I had to leave, balling with tears as I was angry because this is not fair. I enrolled in this program to receive an education, not to get beat up on or made to feel incompetent. Therefore, I had to remove myself from all the noise that was overwhelming me. I had to allow myself some time so that I may return to school in the morning refreshed and rejuvenated.

WEEK 36– POWER OF P-M-S STUDY
Get me away from this noise!

PRAISE: Thank you Lord for reminding me during the night, that weeping may endure for a night, but joy comes in the morning.

MEDITATION: Whenever life seems overwhelming, remove yourself from the noise to focus on the new morning that will begin with JOY!

The Power of P-M-S: Praise-Meditation-Study

STUDY: *~Psalms 30:5~For his anger endureth but a moment, in his favour is life: weeping may endure for a night, but joy cometh in the morning*

STEPS

Do not let anger consume your life with noise that prevents you from waking up with a renewed joy. Before the night's end, write down the joys that will greet you when you rise with a new day!

_____

_____

_____

_____

_____

_____

Alicia Middleton

WEEK 37
~ (John 15:2) ~
Every branch in me that bears no fruit he cuts away, and every branch that does bear fruit he prunes to make it bear even more.

This morning as I reflect on where God has brought me…all I can say is "Hallelujah". It was not until this year that I reconnected with old friends and made new friends. In my life, I've experienced depression and loneliness. I've had failed relationships, friendships, and family outcasts. Oftentimes, I blamed myself and thought it was my fault. I keep questioning, "What is wrong with me, why can't I get along with others?" And the BIG QUESTION, "Why can't I keep a man?" My eyes filled up with tears, whenever I think of the many labels given to me such as Nerd, Conceited, Prideful, Too Independent, Weird and this list can go on. All I can say is God gave me the courage to stand up and continue pressing towards His destiny.

The Power of P-M-S: Praise-Meditation-Study

It was during these times that I realized God was pruning me by picking and separating the unfruitful vines in my life. It was during these times that I had to accept that I am like no other and because I'm like no other, others are intimidated because of their insecurities. It was during these times that I'd come to realize that because of this, I will repel those who are of no use to me in the direction I am going. I had to stop blaming myself and begin PRAISING God because He is doing His Thang in my life.

It hurts when relationships end, but when God says it's Time...It's Time! As you begin to move to levels that very few accomplish, just know that there will be times when the people you thought were with you for life…are no longer there. You will have nights filled with tears but know God is cutting off the branches that bear you no fruit.

WEEK 37 – POWER OF P-M-S STUDY

It's Pruning Time!

Alicia Middleton

PRAISE: Thank you for pruning my vineyard so that my harvest stays fresh!

MEDITATION: Oh Lord, I trust you as you prune away!

STUDY: *~John 15:2 ~ Every branch in me that bears no fruit he cuts away, and every branch that does bear fruit he prunes to make it bear even more.*

STEPS

Keep your eyes stayed on Him and trust me when I say, "There's Joy on the other side, we just have to go through the process of pruning to GET there. Stay strong and keep the faith.

Write some words of encouragement as you go through the processes in your life!

_____

_____

_____

_____

The Power of P-M-S: Praise-Meditation-Study

Alicia Middleton

WEEK 38

~ (Psalm 17:8) ~
Keep me as the apple of the eye, hide me under the shadow of thy wings,

This weekend I celebrate thirty years since I graduated from high school and will be attending a conference where I will network with leaders and professionals in the field of innovative public education. As I am developing and transitioning, I make no excuses for who God designed me to be. I talk different, I walk different, I view different, and I do not seek to win any popularity contests. In the sight of others, I may even be peculiar, but I AM THE APPLE OF GOD'S EYE!

As I press forward, I notice the sensitivity that I've developed in my lifetime through interacting with others. Many friendships were gained, and many were lost, but today I stand confident knowing that these experiences were necessary for my growth and development.

The Power of P-M-S: Praise-Meditation-Study

My regimen is to consistently evaluate myself. I do not blame nor accept blame when things are less than perfect. However, I assess and make the necessary changes within myself. After all, I'm the only one that I can change.

You must know that you are the apple of God's eye and THAT'S ALL THAT MATTERS as you continue to GET what is rightfully yours!

WEEK 38– POWER OF P-M-S STUDY

I AM WHO I AM!

PRAISE: I thank you for making me into the wonderful person I am!

MEDITATION: I continually pray for guidance and direction in loving the beautiful me!

STUDY: *~Psalm 17:8~ Keep me as the apple of the eye, hide me under the shadow of thy wings,*

Alicia Middleton

STEPS

I challenge you to accept who you were, who you are and who you will become no matter how peculiar it appears to others...either they will accept you or they won't. Make a list of your unique and beautiful qualities that you possess!

_____

_____

_____

_____

_____

_____

_____

_____

_____

_____

The Power of P-M-S: Praise-Meditation-Study

WEEK 39

~ (Romans 12: 17, 19) ~
Do not repay anyone evil for evil. Be careful to do what is right in the eyes of everybody. Do not take revenge, my friends, but leave room for God's wrath, for it is written: "It is mine to avenge; I will repay" says the Lord

It was on the Fourth of July, 2014, when I the truly understood the meaning of this passage. My daughter went to an Independence Day Celebration at our local park with her friends. When it was over, she called me to pick her up. I informed her that I was two minutes away. Her friend's mother insisted on driving her home. My daughter informed me that this woman appeared intoxicated. So I told this woman that I was two minutes away and that my daughter must wait for my arrival. Her response was, "You are bugging, I am bringing your daughter with me, and you must come to my house to pick her up," and abruptly hung up the phone. A few minutes later, the woman called to tell me that they are at the local supermarket and I could get her there. I drove to the entrance of the market and my daughter called to inform me that she was in the bathroom trying to escape from this woman. I told her that I was at the entrance and to come out. My daughter entered the car, and the woman appeared on the passenger's side demanding that I get out of the car to talk. I noticed she was intoxicated, so I told her that I did not want to talk and tried pulling off. She began hitting my car preventing my automatic door from closing. As a result, I had to stop and get out of the van to close it manually. As soon as I got out, this woman ran and punched me in the face insisting that she is going to deal with me. I ran into my car to retrieve my phone to call the cops for assistance. I felt helpless as my children observed their mother being assaulted.

This was a moment that defined my inner strength by not taking this matter into my own hands as it could have made matters worse. I could have ended up in jail or dead. This taught me the meaning of allowing the Lord to fight MY battles as his vengeance is mightier.

WEEK 39– POWER OF P-M-S STUDY
YOUR STRENGTH COMES WHEN YOU GIVE IT TO GOD!

The Power of P-M-S: Praise-Meditation-Study

PRAISE: Thank you Lord for giving me the wisdom to turn my situations over to you!

MEDITATION: Teach me O Lord that every battle belongs to You and You will provide vengeance on my behalf.

STUDY: *~ (Romans 12: 17, 19) ~Do not repay anyone evil for evil. Be careful to do what is right in the eyes of everybody. Do not take revenge, my friends, but leave room for God's wrath, for it is written: "It is mine to avenge; I will repay" says the Lord*

STEPS

What matters will you turn over to God to avenge on your behalf?

_____

_____

_____

_____

Alicia Middleton

The Power of P-M-S: Praise-Meditation-Study

WEEK 40

~ (Isaiah 41:10) ~
Fear not for I am with you, Be not dismayed, for I am your God, I will strengthen you, Yes, I will help you, I will uphold you with My righteous hand.

Many times, the struggle is not because of you or because you are doing something wrong. God is preparing and polishing you to shine. So, when you know you are doing all that you can...Stand through it! Lean on God for strength...Focus on His promises, not your problems and know that you are a victor, not a victim!

WEEK 40– POWER OF P-M-S STUDY

FOCUS ON GOD'S PROMISES, NOT YOUR PROBLEMS.

PRAISE: I praise You for Your Promises that wipes out my Problems!

MEDITATION: Teach me about Your promises that are given to me!

Alicia Middleton

<u>STUDY:</u> *~Isaiah 41:10 ~Fear not for I am with you, Be not dismayed, for I am your God, I will strengthen you, Yes, I will help you, I will uphold you with My righteous hand.*

STEPS

List the promises of God that you will focus on today!

_____

_____

_____

_____

_____

_____

_____

_____

The Power of P-M-S: Praise-Meditation-Study

WEEK 41

~ (Proverbs 18:16) ~
A man's gift makes room for him and brings him before great men.

As I began entering my 20th year of service within the NYC Department of Education, many changes were beginning to take place. Many big public schools were closing so that smaller schools could be placed within the school's building. Principals were gaining control of their school budgets. Most new schools were beginning with limited funds forcing them to seek new employees at the beginning of the salary scale. As a result, many tenured employees had to begin to seek employment in other districts. As two new schools entered my building, I became excited about the change as I believed it would bring innovation. Unfortunately, I was at the top of the salary scale and was informed that the schools could not afford my salary despite the talent I brought to the school. This began the whirlwind of my Open House transfer seeking a new school that could afford my salary. This process took a toll on my health and well-being as I had to leave a place where I provided 20+ years of service, but God reminded me that He would strategically place me among Great Men/Women where my innovative gifts in education and ministry will thrive.

WEEK 41– POWER OF P-M-S STUDY
MY GIFTS WILL THRIVE!

PRAISE: Thank You Lord for placing me among greatness!

MEDITATION: Direct me to the place where my talents will thrive.

STUDY: *~Proverbs 18:16~ A man's gift makes room for him and brings him before great men.*

STEPS

Your gifts will pave the way towards greatness and place you where you need to be. Therefore, if you are in constant strife, ensure that your next move aligns with God's

The Power of P-M-S: Praise-Meditation-Study

plan for you! Make a list! Pray over it and He shall direct your next move!

_____

_____

_____

_____

_____

_____

_____

_____

_____

_____

_____

Alicia Middleton

WEEK 42

~ *(Romans 12:18)* ~
Do everything on your part to live in peace with everybody.

As I am getting re-acclimated back into working after being ill for almost four years, this transition is unbelievable. I've completed my coursework in the doctorate program. I am so thankful to God for where He has brought me. As a result, I decided to celebrate after many years of being home-ridden. In attendance was my family and friends but I was overwhelmed by the support of the community. It took me by surprise to see so many at my home to celebrate with me!

Of course, you have those who will try and rain on your parade to spoil it! It's amazing how my neighbors know me by name, address and phone number. Each time I see them, I greet them with a smile to wish them a good day. I have never been confrontational, AND I have never had a celebration of this magnitude. My question is why did some neighbors called

The Power of P-M-S: Praise-Meditation-Study

the police as I celebrated an occasion such as this. It was only nine pm, whatever happened to the meaning of neighborly and living in peace with your neighbors.

WEEK 42– POWER OF P-M-S STUDY

UNITY begins with U-N-I (You and I)!

PRAISE: Thank You for allowing me the ability to build UNITY in the COMMUNITY!

MEDITATION: Please direct me on the path so that my community is united and I'm living in peace with everyone!

STUDY: *~Romans 12:18~Do everything on your part to live in peace with everybody.*

STEPS

God holds you accountable for the things that you do, NOT what others do to you!

List some ways you will help to create peace in your neighboring community.

Alicia Middleton

The Power of P-M-S: Praise-Meditation-Study

WEEK 43

~ (Matthews 6:24) ~
No man can serve two masters: for either he will hate the one, and love the other; or else he will hold to the one, and despise the other. Ye cannot serve God and mammon.

This morning, God is reminding me of the direction HE has chosen for me. He has called me to minister the Word of God in all I say and do; by the words that proceed from my mouth and by my actions. If my words and/or my actions are unbecoming, then I am losing focus of this call and my Christian identity as a minister of God!

As I transition through the many phases of my life, God is positioning me to serve Him and Him only. He is placing me in a leadership position to be an example of Him. When I first received my calling to minister, God spoke to me in a dream where I heard a multitude of people crying for help in a sea that was beginning to consume them. It was then I received His commandment to provide a safe haven of spiritual shelter for them to escape the pain they are receiving from the world.

WEEK 43 – POWER OF P-M-S STUDY

YOU MUST CHOOSE!

PRAISE: Lord I thank You for allowing me the role that will inspire someone to choose YOU!

MEDITATION: Continually fill my heart with the words and inspiration, so I may share with others!

STUDY: *~Matthews 6:24~ No man can serve two masters: for either he will hate the one, and love the other; or else he will hold to the one, and despise the other. Ye cannot serve God and mammon.*

STEPS

You never know what someone is battling and your words can either uplift or tear apart.
Who will you choose to serve this day? Make a list of inspiring words that you will use when encouraging someone to choose God!

The Power of P-M-S: Praise-Meditation-Study

Alicia Middleton

WEEK 44

~ (1 Corinthians 13:1) ~
Though I speak with the tongues of men and of angels, and have not love, I am become as sounding brass, or a tinkling cymbal.
A soft answer turns away wrath: but grievous words stir up anger.

God is reminding me of the safe haven I must provide so that others may escape whatever pain they are in. In communicating with others, I must be mindful of the message I am trying to express. I must ask myself: what message am I trying to communicate and how will I deliver this message. In either of these situations, the original intent of trying to communicate a message will get lost if I use harsh words. If I am to be an example of God's love, I must relate in a tone that can easily be heard. In other words, if I speak with harsh words, it is heard by the other party as a loud sounding noise. The harshness in these words will stir up anger, and the intent of my message will be lost. As a result, the communication has failed.

The Power of P-M-S: Praise-Meditation-Study

WEEK 44– POWER OF P-M-S STUDY

GIVE ME THE TONGUE THAT SPEAKS LOVE!

PRAISE: I thank you for the heart that LOVES!

MEDITATION: Continually feed me with love so that I may share with others!

STUDY: ~1 Corinthians 13:1~ Though I speak with the tongues of men and of angels and have not love, I am become as sounding brass or a tinkling cymbal. A soft answer turns away wrath: but grievous words stir up anger.

Alicia Middleton

STEPS

Your words are the tools you use to love and inspire. Write loving messages to yourself and to someone!

_____

_____

_____

_____

_____

_____

_____

_____

The Power of P-M-S: Praise-Meditation-Study

WEEK 45

~ (Job 33:15) ~
He speaks in dreams, in visions of the night, when deep sleep falls on people as they lie in their beds."

As a minister and Child of God, when I have dreams, God is preparing me for something. I go before HIM in prayer and ask for revelation in HIS word. You have the power to confirm the meaning...yourself. NO ONE ELSE! Can you hear His Voice!

WEEK 45– POWER OF P-M-S STUDY

FILL MY NIGHT WITH VISIONS

PRAISE: Thank you for the night of blissful sleep!

MEDITATION: Give me the revelation of the dream you gave me!

STUDY: *~Job 33:15~ He speaks in dreams, in visions of the night, when deep sleep falls on people as they lie in their beds."*

Alicia Middleton

STEPS

Before going to bed, play a worship song or read one of your favorite scriptural passage. May this fill your sleep with pleasant dreams. When you wake, write the vision and meditate on it. Possibly share it with a loved one!

_____

_____

_____

_____

_____

_____

_____

The Power of P-M-S: Praise-Meditation-Study

WEEK 46

~ (Isaiah 61:1) ~
The Spirit of the Lord God is upon me; because the Lord hath anointed me to preach good tidings unto the meek; he hath sent me to bind up the brokenhearted, to proclaim liberty to the captives, and the opening of the prison to them that are bound.

In 2005, as I lay beside my husband, I awoke to voices of a multitude of people crying for help. I questioned my husband if he heard them. We lived in NYC; our windows were opened, so I thought the voices came from outside, but my husband stated he did not hear them. So I went back to sleep and was awoken by those voices again, but this time, I heard it in the midst of my sleep. I woke my husband, and again he stated, he did not hear them.

I am very selective of who I share this story with as I do not want any false analysis coupled with a diagnosis of being schizophrenic, a sickness that plagues some who are dear to me. I also do not share with most that I often have dreams, visions and hear the voice that often showers me with a blessing. In fact, that's the meaning and development of my entertainment stage name "Madame Raine". The Voice of Showered Blessings, my stage name, was taken from my middle name that my family fondly calls me and the fact that I hear the Voice of Showered Blessings.

Today, I can proudly say that I am Minister Alicia Middleton - Co-Pastor/Founder of

A New Life Ministry, Inc.

WEEK 46 – POWER OF P-M-S STUDY

BE CAREFUL OF THE VOICE YOU LISTEN TO!

PRAISE: Thank you God for giving me the distinction of hearing Your Voice!

MEDITATION: In the midst of my being, it is YOU I will listen to!

STUDY: ~ Isaiah 61:1~The Spirit of the Lord God is upon me; because the Lord hath anointed me to preach good

The Power of P-M-S: Praise-Meditation-Study

tidings unto the meek; he hath sent me to bind up the brokenhearted, to proclaim liberty to the captives, and the opening of the prison to them that are bound.

STEPS

What has God anointed you to do? Make a list and begin implementing them in your life.

_____

_____

_____

_____

_____

_____

_____

Alicia Middleton

WEEK 47

~ (Exodus 9:16) ~
But I have raised you up for this very purpose, that I might show you my power and that my name might be proclaimed in all the earth.

My life has been ordained by God. First, he planted me in a family with a strong desire to serve Him as He knew they would water me well. My grandfather was a Reverend, my parents: a deacon and deaconess. My sister, a college graduate and the first campus I've ever visited to watch her graduate and intern at a middle school. My uncle, an A.M.E. Presiding Elder who served in six of the seven original conferences of the 11th Episcopal District of the State of Florida. I am surrounded by aunts, uncles, cousins, nieces, nephews and family members who are Bishops/Superintendents/Nurses/militia providing service to others.

Today, I am joined with my husband who is an Apostle of A New Life Ministry, Inc. My life and my surroundings taught me the lesson of patience as I watched churches,

The Power of P-M-S: Praise-Meditation-Study

schools, and families being built on the foundation of God's love.

I never realized my true passion until I began to overcome my obstacles. This journey was not easy as I had to learn patience and allow God to open my doors. My past experiences taught me to walk and not run which caused me to trip, hit walls and fall. Despite the fact that I fell, I never allowed myself to fail. I got up, brushed myself off and made sure that I walked while examining the sights surrounding me before making another dash.

I am grateful for every experience along the way, and today as I look in the mirror, I see a future Doctor reflecting back at me!

WEEK 47 – POWER OF P-M-S STUDY

Your Journey teaches you about your destination.

Alicia Middleton

PRAISE: Thank You for allowing me to learn lessons as I travel on my path.

MEDITATION: Please teach me to value the experiences and continually learn lessons from the hiccups of my life.

STUDY: *~Exodus 9:16~ But I have raised you up for this very purpose, that I might show you my power and that my name might be proclaimed in all the earth.*

STEPS

Make a list of lessons that you have learned through your experiences.

_____

_____

_____

_____

_____

_____

The Power of P-M-S: Praise-Meditation-Study

WEEK 48

~ (Romans 12:14) ~
Bless those who persecute you: bless and do not curse them.
I know thy works: behold, I have set before thee an open door, and no man can shut it: for thou hast a little strength, and hast kept my word, and hast not denied my name.

I am just waking up from a dream where I am comforting two women. After sending them a word of encouragement, I began to pray, and God ministered this word to me:

TO BE AN EXTRA BLESSING TO THOSE WHO PURPOSELY TRY TO PERSECUTE ME!

Whatever it is that you are going through, whoever is talking negatively about you, trying to shut a door that God has already opened, PRAY FOR THEM, BLESS THEM AND continue doing what you were called to do.

WEEK 48 – POWER OF P-M-S STUDY

BE A BLESSING, GOD IS IN CONTROL!

Alicia Middleton

PRAISE: Thank you for blessing my enemies!

MEDITATION: I am lifting a prayer of blessing for those who try to curse me!

STUDY: ~Romans 12:14~ *Bless those who persecute you: bless and do not curse them. I know thy works: behold, I have set before thee an open door, and no man can shut it: for thou hast a little strength, and hast kept my word and hast not denied my name.*

STEPS

In what ways can you be a blessing, especially to someone you know is trying to persecute you!

_____

_____

_____

_____

_____

The Power of P-M-S: Praise-Meditation-Study

Alicia Middleton

WEEK 49

*~ (Isaiah 43:19) ~
I will even make a road in the wilderness
And rivers in the desert.*

My life took an unexpectant, amazing turn. At the beginning of 2016, I was offered a Director's position of The Office of Quality Improvement and Career Center. To be honest, I was fretting on how would I be able to pay for my doctorate education and my children's education on a retirement salary. I never verbalized this concern, I simply entered my resume and began applying for positions on Higher Ed. Immediately I was called to interview at colleges in Texas and New Mexico. The College of San Juan gave me an offer I could not refuse.

Making this move will complicate my doctorate research at East Stroudsburg University but I have to consider my son's hard work as he was accepted at Latrobe University in Australia. This was an opportunity that he worked hard to

The Power of P-M-S: Praise-Meditation-Study

achieve. Well as mothers do, I decided to afford my son this opportunity and put my dissertation research on hold.

I am confident that God will make a way!

WEEK 49– POWER OF P-M-S STUDY

HE NEVER FAILED ME YET!

<u>PRAISE:</u> Thank you God for supplying all my needs and making provisions when it all else fails!

<u>MEDITATION:</u> I will patiently wait on You Lord to direct my next moves!

<u>STUDY:</u> ~ *(Isaiah 43:19) ~I will even make a road in the wilderness and rivers in the desert.*

Alicia Middleton

STEPS

What areas in your life do you feel defeated? Make a list and remember God will make a way out of no way!

_____

_____

_____

_____

_____

_____

_____

_____

_____

_____

_____

_____

The Power of P-M-S: Praise-Meditation-Study

WEEK 50
~ *(Isaiah 43: 19)* ~
Behold, I will do a New Thing

Today marks the day that I have completed the manuscript of my personal devotional and will continue to focus on my dissertation research on "Innovative Initiatives in Public Education". My 24+ years working in the New York City Public Education with innovative pioneers: Deborah Meier, Syl Fliegel and John Falco in the schools of East Harlem gave me firsthand experience of this new movement in public education.

My personal experience includes raising a son that is classified as a growing statistic because he is a male being raised without his biological father. He was born with a birthmark that resembled a tear drop which is mistaken by gang members as one of their signs. During his years of schooling, he was often approached by gang members. I knew that the traditional public schooling would not be conducive for his success and growth. As a result, I am thankful for "School Choice" as I was afforded the opportunity to decide what educational program he would attend. Today, I can proudly say that he is an overachieving, Straight A student and the recipient of a full Speedwell Scholarship to represent the USA and the state of PA as a student ambassador studying abroad in the Netherlands during his senior year of high school in hopes to major in International Studies.

I have a beautiful young daughter who exemplifies me in every way. She thrives for long lasting relationships. Her heart is filled with love but being raised without her biological father may have caused her to seek love in the wrong ways. However, I am forever thankful for my husband. Although he is not her biological father, you could never tell her or him that. He provides the love and care a young girl needs as she develops into a young woman.

The Power of P-M-S: Praise-Meditation-Study

WEEK 50 – POWER OF P-M-S STUDY

MY LIFE IS MADE ANEW

PRAISE: Thank you Lord for The Power of P-M-S

Thank you Lord as I continue my journey through this dysfunctional world, I hope to do a "New Thing" and provide innovative initiatives to ensure student success for all. I pray that this devotional will bless and empower all that reads it, to continue on your successful journey towards your Godly divine destination!

you Lord for The Power of P-M-S (Praise-Meditation-Study) as it will forever be my guide on this journey.

MEDITATION: I will continue to talk to You while being still to hear what You have destined me to do!

STUDY: ~Isaiah 43: 18~ Behold, I will do a New Thing

Alicia Middleton

STEPS

Cherish the steps that God is taking you on in your life.

Each day is a New Day with a New Chance to get aligned with Your Purpose!

The Power of P-M-S: Praise-Meditation-Study

Alicia LaRaine Middleton is a retired educator working for 24 years in the New York City public school system devising educational and performing arts programs for middle school students. Her most noted accolades are producing plays entitled "The Sneaker" an urban rendition of Cinderella and "Back in the Days" – The Sounds of Motown.

Alicia relocated to the Poconos Mountains of Pennsylvania and pursued her masters and doctorate education. During this time, she became the founder of Rainey Roo Productions where she hosted Red Carpet events conducting interviews with Derrick Simmons, Rhonda Ross and Sean Nelson. She also starred in the 2006 Tiffany Gospel Award Winning Best Off-Broadway Gospel Play "Freed". She partnered with her husband as Pastors of A New Life Ministry, Inc. and produced Sistah Chat Radio on the 2015 MTV Woodie Award Winning Station
90.3 WESS FM radio, which highlighted diversified women chatting about diversified issues.

Alicia Middleton

Her fondest feat is becoming one of the founders of The Monroe County Image Awards of PA in which community leaders are applauded for their outstanding community service in making the Poconos a place one is proud to call home. This began her advocacy for building communities and will be awarded as Advocate for a Better America at the 2016 Pocono Mountains Film Festival.

Alicia currently resides in Farmington, New Mexico and is the Director of Quality Improvement and Career Center at San Juan College. She has been appointed to the Mayor's Community Relations Commission, Minority Roundtable and will be initiating the first African American Club on campus where she is sponsoring *The First Black History Month Celebration Feb. 2017*.

She is the proud wife of Rev. PK, mother of son Ahrayalab Simon and daughter Alema Isabelle.

www.ingramcontent.com/pod-product-compliance
Lightning Source LLC
LaVergne TN
LVHW051101080426
835508LV00019B/2010